MICROWAVE
COOKING

ESSENTIAL TIPS

MICROWAVE COOKING

EDITORIAL CONSULTANT ON VEGETARIAN COOKERY
Sarah Brown

DORLING KINDERSLEY
London • New York • Stuttgart

A DORLING KINDERSLEY BOOK

Editor Diana Craig
Art Editor Clive Hayball
Managing Editor Mary-Clare Jerram
Managing Art Editor Amanda Lunn
US Editor Laaren Brown
Production Controller Meryl Silbert

First American Edition, 1995
2 4 6 8 10 9 7 5 3 1
Published in the United States by
Dorling Kindersley Publishing, Inc., 95 Madison Avenue,
New York, New York 10016

Published in Great Britain by Dorling Kindersley Limited

ISBN 1-56458-987-0

Computer page makeup by Mark Bracey
Text film output by Graphical Innovations, Great Britain
Reproduced by Colourscan
Printed and bound by Graphicom, Italy

ESSENTIAL TIPS

_____ PAGES 36-54 _____

COOKING
BASIC FOODS

_____ PAGES 55-69 _____

TIMESAVING
TECHNIQUES

UNDERSTAND YOUR MICROWAVE

1 WHY USE A MICROWAVE?

Once you have become familiar with the various cooking techniques, you will find that microwave cooking has several advantages.

- A microwave oven is quick and convenient to use; it can cook foods in a fraction of the time they would take using other methods.
- Microwave cooking is healthy. Because foods cook more quickly than in a conventional oven, the nutrients they contain are better preserved.
- Shorter cooking times mean that there is less risk of food drying up or falling apart.

SAUSAGE & POTATO △
*Produce a quick and tasty
supper with minimum effort.*

BANANA PECAN
BREAD ▷
*Cakes and
breads are
easy to make.*

◁ SPRING VEGETABLES
*Vegetables, cooked in only
a little water, retain more
of their soluble vitamins.*

2 WHAT MICROWAVES WELL?

Microwave cooking produces especially successful results with particular foods.

- Fish microwaves very well, the flesh becoming beautifully moist and flaky.
- Whole fruits and vegetables retain a fresher flavor if they are microwaved.
- Pastry shells bake well empty when covered with absorbent paper and a plate.
- All types of poultry microwave well, but need some additional browning (see p.30).
- Sauces and custards cook with amazing ease; there's no direct heat rising up from underneath to make them stick.

PEARS BELLE HELENE △

◁ SOLE BONNE FEMME

SALMON STEAK △

"BARBECUED" CHICKEN & HONEY-SOY CHICKEN ▷

TOMATO TARTLET △

3 FOODS TO AVOID

Certain cooking techniques and recipes will not work in a microwave oven, so you should not even attempt them.

- Do not try to hard-boil eggs or cook large shellfish. They could explode because of the buildup of steam under their shells.
- Do not microwave batters and pancakes. They will be soft and soggy, rather than crisp and dry.
- Do not try to roast very large turkeys because they cook too unevenly in a microwave.
- Do not cook smoked hams. Their high salt content will make them too dry.
- Do not attempt to deep-fry because you will not be able to control the oil temperature.

BATTER

WHOLE EGGS

CRAB

4 DANGEROUS PRACTICES

A microwave is an invaluable aid when used correctly, but there are certain practices to avoid.

- Never turn your oven on when it is empty; microwaves may bounce off the walls and damage the cavity. In case someone turns the oven on inadvertently, leave a cup of water inside it to absorb the microwaves.
- Never use your oven to dry or to heat clothes, papers, or anything except food.
- Never put undue strain on the door, for example, by hanging towels from it, because this could damage the door. Do not use the oven if the latches or seals on the door look damaged; get them professionally repaired.

DON'T DRY SOCKS IN THE OVEN

5 OVEN WON'T WORK

There are several simple reasons why your oven may not be working; the cause may be an electrical fault, or the oven's safety mechanism may be operating. Check the following:
▪ Make sure that you have closed the door securely. If the door isn't properly shut, the oven is designed not to switch on, for safety reasons.
▪ Check to see whether you have plugged the oven in properly.
▪ Make sure that the fuse hasn't blown, and that there is no power outage occurring.

6 WHY BLUE SPARKS?

If you place an item made of, or containing, metal inside your oven, you can cause sparking or arcing ("blue sparks"). Instead of allowing the microwaves to pass through, the metal reflects them back out into the cavity, causing sparking, and even pitting the oven walls. This in turn will distort the pattern of the microwaves, and so affect the oven's performance; in extreme cases, it may even damage the magnetron. If your oven starts sparking, switch it off at once to avoid damage.

7 FOOD WON'T COOK

If you find that the food you have placed in your microwave isn't cooking, you may have set the oven incorrectly, or you may be using unsuitable cookware (see p.18).
▪ Make sure that you have not set the oven on "timer" or "hold."
▪ If you are cooking food in the packaging in which you bought it – for example, store-bought frozen vegetables, a quiche, or a stew – check that the packaging is not foil. Foil is made of metal, and microwaves cannot pass through it.
▪ Do not use containers made of metallic glazed pottery, because, like metal, this blocks microwave energy and prevents cooking.

FOIL CONTAINERS

METALLIC GLAZED POTTERY

8 COOKS TOO SLOWLY

There are several reasons why food may be cooking too slowly:
- If your oven shares a circuit with another appliance, it may not be operating at full power.
- You may have set the power level of your oven incorrectly.
- The food may have been at the wrong temperature when you put it into the oven. Meat, fish, poultry, and most vegetables should be at refrigerator temperature, canned and dry goods at room temperature.
- If standing time is part of the recipe, you may not have allowed long enough. Standing time is part of the microwave cooking process.

TOO LARGE △
Check that pieces of food are not too large, as this slows cooking.

FINISHING PROCESS ▽
Cover roasts with a foil tent and let stand. This allows the internal temperature to rise so that the meat is fully cooked.

9 COOKS TOO QUICKLY

If you find that food is cooking too fast in your microwave, check the following points:
- The oven's power level may be set too high.
- The oven may have a higher wattage than the recipe requires, so adjust the cooking time.
- A single-setting oven may cook certain foods, such as eggs or cheese, too quickly. Remedy this by placing a microwave-safe bowl containing 2 cups (500 ml) water in the oven. The water will attract microwave energy and slow cooking.

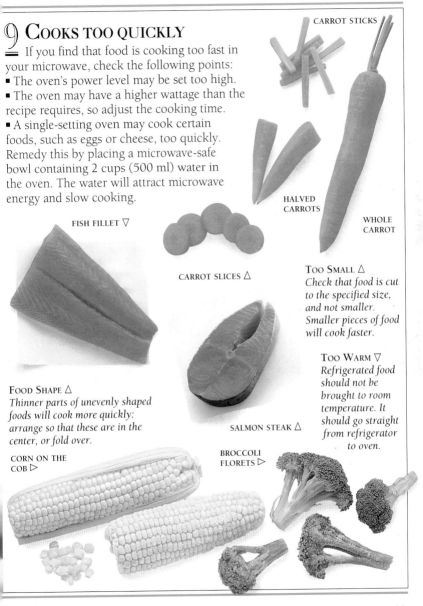

CARROT STICKS

HALVED CARROTS

WHOLE CARROT

FISH FILLET ▽

CARROT SLICES △

TOO SMALL △
Check that food is cut to the specified size, and not smaller. Smaller pieces of food will cook faster.

TOO WARM ▽
Refrigerated food should not be brought to room temperature. It should go straight from refrigerator to oven.

SALMON STEAK △

FOOD SHAPE △
Thinner parts of unevenly shaped foods will cook more quickly: arrange so that these are in the center, or fold over.

CORN ON THE COB ▷

BROCCOLI FLORETS ▷

10 COOKING UNEVENLY

If microwaves are not reaching all parts of the food at the same rate, the food will cook unevenly. Try the following checks and remedies:
- Make sure that the air vent is not blocked, and that there is nothing heavy on top of the oven.
- Prop up the dish to raise it off the oven floor so that microwaves can reach the food evenly, from the bottom of the dish as well as the sides.
- Rotate, rearrange, or stir food during cooking so that it does not stay in the same "hot spots," where there is a greater concentration of energy.
- Try to ensure that foods are of uniform size – thinner parts will cook more quickly. Place them in the middle, where cooking is slower.

FIND THE HOT SPOTS
Place bowls of water in the oven and heat on High. The hottest spots are where the water bubbles first.

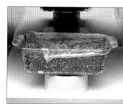

PLACE ON A RAMEKIN △
If you do not have a rack, use a ramekin or plate to lift foods off the oven floor.

◁ **USE A RACK**
Elevate dishes by placing them on a microwave-safe rack or trivet.

11 CONVERT COOKING TIMES

If you want to use a recipe that does not give alternative timings for ovens with different wattages, use the following conversion guide. For a recipe intended for a 600-watt oven, reduce the length of cooking time by 10 seconds per minute if you are using a 700-watt machine. If you have a 500-watt oven, increase it by 15 seconds per minute. Check frequently, however, to make sure that the food is not overcooking.

OVEN TIMER

12 CLEANING KNOW-HOW

If you get into the habit of always wiping your oven after use, it will be much easier to keep clean.

- Remove spills – they may absorb microwave energy and consequently slow cooking.
- Before you clean the touch control panel, open the door or you may switch the oven on.
- Clean a carousel or a combination oven according to the manufacturer's instructions.

SOFT SPONGES

1 Wipe with a clean cloth or sponge dipped in a mild detergent or diluted dishwashing liquid. Rinse and dry.

2 Make sure that you clean the door seal thoroughly: this is where small pieces of food are often trapped.

3 Rub off cooked-on food with a plastic scourer (never steel wool), or soften it with steam by boiling water in the oven.

13 DEODORIZE YOUR MICROWAVE

To remove lingering cooking odors from your oven, air it occasionally by leaving the door ajar, and wipe over the inside with baking soda dissolved in warm water.

Deodorize your oven using the following recipe. In a 1-quart (1-liter) cup or bowl, combine 1 cup (250 ml) warm water with a few sprigs of thyme, or 2 lemon slices, or 2 teaspoons of mixed spice. Heat on High for 3 minutes, or until the mixture is boiling, then remove to leave a fresh-smelling oven.

DEODORIZING MIXTURE

EQUIPMENT

14 COOKING EQUIPMENT TO USE

Many ordinary items of cookware can be used in the microwave, provided they contain no metal: these include glass-ceramic, porcelain, pottery, and ovenproof glass bowls, dishes and casseroles. Strong plastic containers marked dishwasher-safe and designed to withstand high temperatures are suitable too. For heating foods, you can even use wooden or straw containers, but only leave them in the oven briefly or they may split.

OVENPROOF GLASS ▽
You can safely use ovenproof glass for normal cooking and heating, provided it is metal-free. For cooking at high temperatures, only use glass that is microwave-safe.

PORCELAIN & CHINA △
Sturdy porcelain and china containers, with no metal content, are suitable for microwaving. Plates are handy when cooking for one and make useful lids.

PLASTICS & PAPER △
Use paper towels and rigid, dishwasher-safe plastic for heating foods briefly. For covering foods, use waxed paper, or microwave-safe plastic wrap.

POTTERY △
Use glazed, metal-free stoneware and pottery for cooking as well as heating. If you want to heat food for short periods, you can also use wicker, another natural material.

◁ **GLASS-CERAMIC**
Cook and heat foods in glass-ceramic dishes. For cooking at high temperatures, they should be marked microwave-safe.

15 COOKING EQUIPMENT TO AVOID

Containers made of certain materials should never be used in a microwave oven; not only will they interfere with the normal cooking processes, but they may also damage your oven. The main materials you should avoid are metal, which can cause arcing (*see p.11*), unglazed pottery, certain plastics, and recycled paper, which may contain metal.

POTTERY ▷
Avoid pottery or earthenware that is not fully glazed, both inside and outside, or it may absorb moisture from the food and interfere with the cooking. If the glaze is metallic, however, do not use the container.

MELAMINE & POLYSTYRENE △
Do not use plastics such as melamine and polystyrene, because these may overheat and break. Do not cook fat- or sugar-rich foods in plastic, since fat and sugar can make plastic melt.

METALS & FOILS △
*Do not place items made
of, or containing, metal
in your oven, unless your
instruction book tells you
how to use them, or they
are marked microwave-
safe. When shielding food
with foil, keep the foil at
least 1 in (2.5 cm) away
from the oven's walls.*

CHINA & GLASS ▷
*Avoid china and
glass that has
decorative gold
or silver trim. Also
avoid lead crystal and
glass or china that has
been repaired with glue.*

19

16 SPECIAL COOKWARE

Many items of cookware are specially designed
for use in the microwave oven and are widely available.
They are generally made from materials that allow the
microwaves to pass through to heat the food inside,
and include a wide selection of containers such as cake
and loaf pans, ramekins, baking molds, and stacking
containers for reheating foods. You can use many of them
in the freezer as well as the microwave, which means that
you can cook, freeze, and defrost food in the same dish.

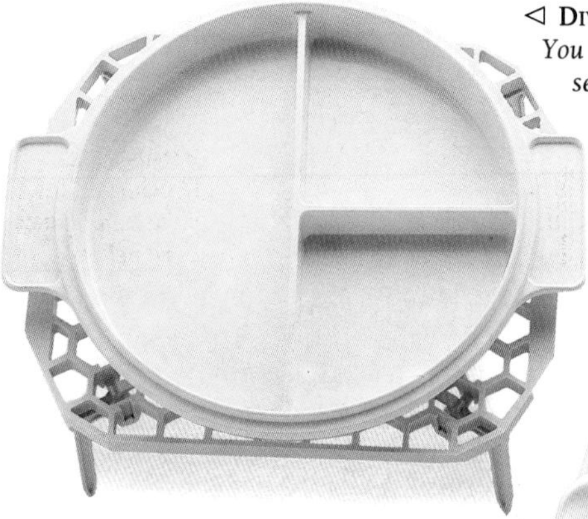

◁ **DIVIDED DISH**
*You can heat or cook
several foods at
once in this
dish. Use the
rack to raise
baked foods
or casseroles.*

**PLASTIC
SPOONS** △
*Leave in
food for stirring.
You can also use
the ladle for
serving food.*

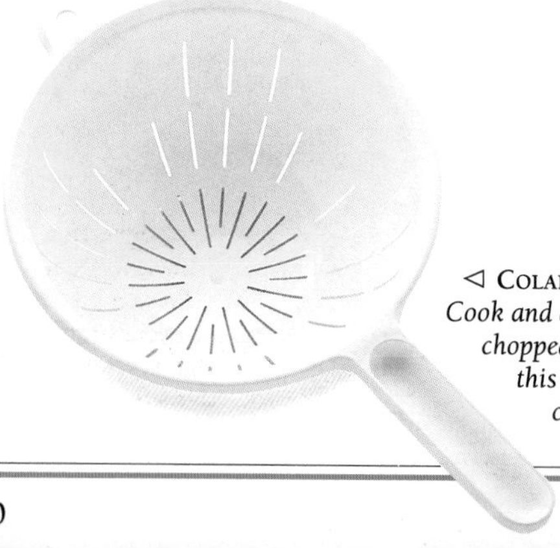

◁ **COLANDER**
*Cook and drain
chopped meat in
this plastic
colander.*

GLASS-LIDDED DISH △
*Use the dish for oven-
to-table serving. Rotate
food on the carousel so
that it cooks evenly.*

◁ **BUN DISH**
Bake small cakes and buns in this dish. You can also use it for poaching eggs.

LOAF PAN △
This is ideal for cooking cakes, meat loaves, and pâtés.

RAMEKINS △
Poach eggs and bake small cakes in ramekins.

RIDGED MOLD △
Bake cakes and custards in this ring mold.

PLASTIC BUNDT PAN △
Cook cakes, casseroles, and meat loaves in this pan.

ROASTING DISH WITH RACK ▷
This allows meat and chicken juices to drain.

◁ **NONSTICK BAKING DISH**
Roast meats and cook casseroles and vegetables in this baking dish.

BROWNING DISH △
Use to brown meats and fish.

17 THE BEST CONTAINER SHAPES

Food cooks more evenly in round dishes than it does in square or rectangular ones; in the latter, the corners receive more microwave energy and so food here tends to cook faster. Bundt pans are the ideal shape because they allow microwaves to reach food in the center as quickly as the sides. Choose deep bowls if cooking in fast-boiling water, and make sure containers are large enough for certain foods to swell.

ROUND DISH FOR EVENLY COOKED FOOD

18 IMPROVISE CONTAINERS

If you do not have the right kind of container, make your own.
- Cardboard boxes are useful for baking cakes. Line the box with waxed paper before adding the cake mixture. Avoid boxes with metal trimmings; metal blocks microwaves. Do not use any that have coatings because the hot food may melt them.
- If you create a bundt pan with a dish and a tumbler (*see right*), hold the tumbler in place while you fill the dish with food.

IMPROVISED BUNDT PAN
Stand a glass tumbler in a round dish for an easily improvised bundt pan.

19 HOW TO TEST CONTAINERS

To find out whether a dish is suitable for the microwave, place it in the oven with a cup or bowl containing 1 cup (300 ml) cold water. Heat on High for 1 minute. If the dish stays cool and the water is hot, the dish is suitable. If the water is still cool and the dish hot, do not use it. The dish contains moisture that will attract microwave energy away from the food.

CUP-OF-WATER TEST

20 ROASTING BAGS

These are especially good for cooking meat and poultry because they help it to brown. You will still need to raise the meat on a rack to keep it out of its cooking juices, so place the rack inside the bag and not underneath. Pierce the bag to allow steam to escape. If the bag is too small, cut it open along one side, and arrange it like a tent.

MEAT IN A ROASTING BAG

21 THERMOMETERS

To check on the internal temperature of meat and see how it is cooking, insert a microwave-safe thermometer into the meat halfway through the cooking time. Leave it in the meat, so you can check the temperature through the glass door.

■ Use a thermometer to test the temperature during standing time, when the meat finishes cooking. At this time, the internal temperature may rise by 41–46° F (5–8° C).

■ Use a conventional metal meat thermometer out of the oven, when the meat is standing.

CONVENTIONAL MEAT THERMOMETER

ESSENTIAL COOKING TIPS

22 COVER FOOD

There are various reasons for covering food before you cook it in the microwave.

- It keeps fat from the hot food from being spattered over the walls of the oven.
- It results in faster and more even cooking. The heat of the steam, combined with the action of the microwaves, speeds the process.
- It creates steam, which tenderizes food and keeps it moist. Cover soups, stews, less tender meats, thicker pieces of fish, and vegetables, but do not cover "dry" foods, such as cookies.

PAPER TOWELS △
Lay these over fatty foods to prevent grease spatters and to absorb excess fat.

PLATES △
If a dish has no lid, use a plain plate instead. It should cover the dish completely.

◁ LIDS & COVERS
For foods that need stirring or checking, a microwave-safe lid is the most practical cover.

23 WRAP FOOD

The microwave process brings out the moisture content of foods so, if you want some foods, such as baked potatoes, to retain a dry surface, wrap them in absorbent paper towels before placing them in the oven to cook. The paper will soak up the excess moisture.

- Heat bread rolls in a basket lined with paper or cotton napkins. The napkins will prevent soggy crusts, and you can serve the rolls in the basket.
- Always remove paper as soon as you've taken the food from the oven, or the paper may stick.

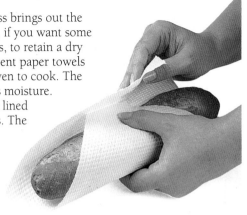

WRAP CRUSTY BREAD

24 LINE DISHES

To prevent the contents from sticking to cake pans and baking dishes, line the containers before filling them with the uncooked mixture. Use paper towels or waxed paper, or nonstick baking parchment, for cake dishes. Remove the paper after standing time to keep it from sticking to the cake. Do not grease cake pans or coat with flour; this leaves a film on the cake.

PLASTIC WRAP △
Use plastic wrap for pâtés, meat loaves, and terrines.

◁ **PAPER TOWEL**
Cut paper to fit the dish before adding the contents.

NONSTICK BAKING PARCHMENT ▷
This is easy to peel off the cake base.

25 HOW TO ARRANGE FOOD

A microwave oven heats the center of a dish more slowly than the edge, so you must place food carefully for even cooking.
- If food is unevenly shaped, arrange it so that more delicate parts are in the center, and denser, thicker parts near the edge.
- Arrange foods of equal size in a circle around the edge, spacing them out evenly so that microwaves can reach all sides.
- Make sure that food is an even depth, spreading it out if necessary.

DENSER PARTS NEAR THE EDGE

26 PIERCE FOODS

Steam can build up considerably during microwaving, so you should pierce any foods that have a tight-fitting "skin" or membrane to keep them from bursting while cooking.
- Pierce the skin of whole vegetables and fruit with a fork, or with the tip of a sharp knife.
- Use a toothpick to pierce the membrane that covers egg yolks, chicken livers, or oysters.
- Do not pierce whole fish, but slash it across the thickest part on both sides.

CASINGS △
Sausages and other foods with casings must be pierced before you cook them in the microwave.

◁ **MEMBRANES**
Pierce the membranes of egg yolks, chicken livers, and oysters.

OUTER SKINS ▷
Vegetables such as potatoes, tomatoes, and bell peppers need piercing to release steam.

27 SHIELD FOOD

To prevent delicate or thin areas of food – such as the bony ends of roasts of meat, or the heads and tails of large fish – from overcooking, shield them with small, smooth strips of aluminum foil for part of the cooking time.

- The amount of food left uncovered must be greater than that shielded by the foil.
- Secure the strips well. Wooden toothpicks make effective "ties."
- If any foil becomes loose, switch off the power and remove the loose piece.

SHIELD EXPOSED BONES

28 WHY YOU SHOULD STIR FOOD

Microwaves penetrate food to a depth of only about 2 in (5 cm), so that denser foods, and food in the center of the dish that is farther from the source of energy, cook more slowly. To make sure that all parts of the food receive the same amount of microwave energy, stir frequently during cooking, bringing food from the center to the edge, and from the edge inward. To remind yourself to stir, set your oven timer to go off at regular intervals.

STIR A CASSEROLE

29 TURN & ROTATE

Certain solid foods that cannot be stirred will need turning instead.

- Give baked dishes such as lasagne a quarter- or half-turn at intervals during cooking, rotating in one direction only.
- Turn over thick, dense pieces of food, being cooked on their own or in liquid.

TURN FISH CAKES

30 REARRANGE FOOD

Microwave energy cannot reach all parts of the food at the same time, so you should rearrange foods that cannot be stirred to avoid leaving them in the same hot spot during the whole cooking time. Move items from the edge of the dish, which heats more quickly, to the center, and from the back to the front. When rearranging foods such as hamburgers or baked potatoes, you can turn them over, too.

CORN ON THE COB

31 WHY FOOD MUST STAND

Microwaved foods continue to cook by internal heat after you remove them from the oven, or after you switch the power off, so letting the food stand is part of the cooking process. Some foods, such as cakes, may look uncooked when they come out of the oven, but will firm up and dry out after standing.

Food cooks more slowly in the center in the microwave, so taking it from the oven before it is fully cooked and letting it stand allows the center to finish cooking without overcooking the edges.

Standing times vary; as a general rule, the denser the food, the longer the standing time you should allow.

LIGHTLY COOKED EGGS
Remove scrambled eggs from the oven when they are just past the runny stage.

LET EGG SET
After 1–2 minutes, the egg will be set and will resemble conventionally cooked egg.

32 TENTING TECHNIQUE

Roasts, whole birds, and large fish require a long standing time to finish cooking. To keep them hot during this time, cover them with a tent of foil, shiny side inward. Make sure that you arrange the foil loosely; if it is too tight, the food will begin to steam, and this will affect its taste and texture. Loosely covered meat will also shrink less.

COVER MEAT LOOSELY WITH FOIL

33 USE A BROWNING DISH

Because microwave energy cooks food so quickly, the fat in the food does not become hot enough to caramelize on the surface. As a result, microwaved meat and poultry can look quite pale and unpalatable. To remedy this when cooking poultry parts or smaller cuts of meat, use a browning dish. Made from, or coated with, a special material that absorbs microwave energy and reaches around 425° F (220° C), the dish will both cook the food and brown it at the same time.

MICROWAVE BROWNING DISH

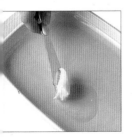

1 Preheat the dish, according to the instructions. When it is hot, add margarine, butter, or oil as required.

2 Place a chicken piece on the melted fat or hot oil, pressing it down with a spatula. Cook until the underside is brown.

3 Turn the chicken over, holding it with tongs. Cook until the other side is brown and the juices run clear.

34 BROWNING AGENT IDEAS

Meat and poultry cooked in the microwave need a little extra help to achieve the same golden finish they would have if cooked conventionally. One solution is to brown these foods in a special browning dish (see p.29). If you do not have this piece of equipment, however, or if the piece of meat you are cooking is too large to be browned in such a way, there are various coatings and sauces that you can sprinkle or brush on, or rub in, to produce a similar effect. Some will also give the meat added texture and flavor.

MICROWAVE BROWNING
Sprinkle this special coating on meat and poultry before cooking.

GOLDEN CHICKEN ▽
Whole chickens can look especially pale when they are cooked by microwave. For crisp-looking, golden birds, use a suitable browning agent.

35 WHEN IS FOOD COOKED?

Microwaved food may look different from conventionally cooked food when you remove it from the oven, so there are a few points to bear in mind when checking to see if it is cooked.

■ Make sure you have allowed enough standing time. Food can look underdone when you take it from the oven, but will be cooked after standing for the time specified in the recipe.

■ Always undercook rather than overcook: you can easily return food to the oven.

■ If you are cooking individual portions, test each separately to see if it is ready.

OY OR BARBECUE SAUCE
ub barbecue or soy sauce
to uncooked poultry skin to
ve it a golden color.

MARMALADE
Jse marmalade to glaze ham
fter cooking; coat chicken
alfway through.

GRAVY BROWNING
Brush meat and poultry with
ravy browning before you
ook it in the microwave.

TESTING CUSTARD △
A knife inserted halfway
between the center and
edge should come
out clean.

TESTING MEAT △
You should be able to pierce
a fork through a small piece
or cube.

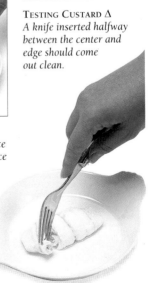

TESTING FISH ▷
The flesh should
be opaque and
should separate
easily when flaked
with a fork.

36 HOW TO DEFROST FOOD

Most microwave ovens have a Defrost control, but if your oven does not have this feature, you can simulate it by repeatedly turning the power to High for 30 seconds, then off for 1½ minutes, until the food is almost defrosted. Remove food and let stand to thaw fully, or the edges will start to cook.

CHICKEN MARENGO

- Defrost food in a tight-fitting container. If food has too much room, it will spread as it melts and start to cook at the edges.
- Break food up as it defrosts, rearranging or stirring it to bring it from the edge to the center. Give pies, cakes, and other baked dishes a quarter-turn every minute or so.
- Place breads, cakes, and pastry on paper towels so they can absorb excess moisture.
- Pierce bags of food to prevent bursting.

CHEESE & CHILI CHAPATIS

37 HOW TO DEFROST MEAT

Set your oven to Defrost or Medium-Low to defrost meat, or turn the oven on and off to allow the temperature to even out.

- Place roasts and larger cuts of meat on a microwave-safe rack in a microwave-safe dish when you defrost them; if the meat rests in its own juices, it will start to cook.
- Cover meat loosely with waxed or greaseproof paper. This will retain heat, and so speed defrosting.

◁ **BURGERS**
When sufficiently thawed, separate and arrange in a single layer on a rack.

MEAT CUBES ▷
Separate and space cubes out in a dish, removing individual cubes as they defrost.

38 DEFROST POULTRY

Loosen or remove wrappings first, or they will trap heat, and the poultry will begin to cook.
- Set your microwave to Defrost or Medium-Low. For poultry parts, allow 6–7 minutes per 1 lb (450 g). Whole birds will need 5–9 minutes for every 1 lb (450 g).

- Incompletely defrosted poultry can cause food poisoning. To make sure a whole bird is fully thawed, soak it in a bowl of cold water for up to 30 minutes after defrosting to dissolve any ice left in the cavity. Leave poultry pieces to stand for 5 minutes to thaw bony parts fully.

1 Place a whole bird on a rack in a dish to allow the juices to drain. If left in the juices, the bird will begin to cook.

2 Halfway through, turn the bird breast side down. Cover it with greaseproof or waxed paper to keep it warm.

3 Toward the end of defrosting, remove paper and turn bird over. Shield any warm spots with smooth foil.

39 DEFROST FISH

Set your oven to Defrost or Medium-Low, and defrost fish for 6–9 minutes per 1 lb (450 g).
- Turn whole fish over during the defrosting time; rearrange fish fillets.
- To keep thinner parts of whole fish from starting to cook, shield with foil after you turn the fish.
- Cover whole fish and defrost, then stand so that the internal temperature can even out to complete the thawing.
- If the cavity of a whole fish is still icy, rinse it under cold running water.

SHIELD DELICATE AREAS WITH FOIL

40 DEFROST SHELLFISH

Frozen shellfish defrosts very quickly in the microwave, but take care that it does not start to cook: it should feel pliable but still cold.

- Defrost small quantities or blocks of frozen shellfish, such as crabmeat, in the package. Place larger quantities in a shallow, microwave-safe dish.
- Cover and defrost large shellfish, then let stand to equalize the internal temperature and thaw fully.
- Cook shellfish as soon as possible after it has defrosted to prevent the growth of harmful bacteria.

SEPARATE SHELLFISH TO SPEED DEFROSTING

41 HOW TO REHEAT FOOD

Fast microwave heating times mean that foods reheated in a microwave still look and taste as if they have been freshly cooked. They also retain more vitamins than if they were reheated conventionally.

- Foods in sauce reheat better than "dry" foods, but do not put them in too large a container or the sauce will spread and dry out at the edges.
- Reheat casseroles more quickly by placing them in a shallow dish and spreading them out in an even layer.
- Cover dry foods, such as pastry, with paper towels to absorb moisture.

APPLE & CRANBERRY TART

42 WHAT CAN I BLANCH?

You should blanch most vegetables and some fruits before freezing them to stop enzyme activity that causes loss of color, flavor, and texture. To blanch 1 lb (450 g) of vegetables or fruit, place in a bowl with 3 tablespoons water, cover, and cook on High for the times given below. Stir once. Drain, plunge into ice water, drain, and freeze.

CUT INTO EVEN-SIZED PIECES

43 HOW LONG DO I BLANCH?

Blanch vegetables and fruits for the following times before freezing.

Microwave time on High in minutes

	500 W oven	600 W oven	700 W oven
Apples	3–5 mins	3–4 mins	2–3 mins
Asparagus	5 mins	4 mins	3 mins
Beet (small)	6 mins	5 mins	4 mins
Bell peppers (sliced)	3½ mins	3 mins	2½ mins
Broccoli (florets)	3–5 mins	2½–4 mins	2–3 mins
Brussels Sprouts	6 mins	5 mins	4 mins
Carrots	4 mins	3½ mins	3 mins
Cauliflower (florets)	3½ mins	3 mins	2½ mins
Corn	3½ mins	3 mins	2½ mins
Corn on the cob (2)	8½ mins	7 mins	6 mins
Fava Beans	3½ mins	3 mins	2½ mins
Green Beans (whole)	3½ mins	3 mins	2½ mins
Green Beans (sliced)	2½ mins	2 mins	1½ mins
Leeks (sliced)	2½–3 mins	2–2½ mins	1½–2 mins
Onions (sliced)	2½ mins	2 mins	1½ mins
Parsnips	3½ mins	3 mins	2½ mins
Pears	3–5 mins	3–4 mins	2–3 mins
Peas	3–5 mins	2 mins	1½ mins
Rhubarb	3–5 mins	3–4 mins	2–3 mins
Spinach	2½ mins	2 mins	1½ mins
Zucchini	3½ mins	3 mins	2½ mins

COOKING BASIC FOODS

44 BRASSICAS

Prepare these vegetables as for conventional cooking. To preserve flavor and crispness, cook briefly in a small amount of water.

◁ CABBAGE
Shred and place in a dish with 2 tbsp (30 ml) water, but omit water for young green cabbage. Cook, adding an extra 2 minutes for red cabbage. Stand 2–4 minutes.

CAULIFLOWER △
Cover florets and cook in 2–3 tbsp (30–45 ml) water. Stand 2–3 minutes.

BROCCOLI △
Trim, cover, and cook in 2 tbsp (30 ml) water. Stand 3 minutes.

BRUSSELS SPROUTS ▷
Cut a cross in each base, then place in a dish. Add 2 tbsp (30 ml) water, cover, and cook. Allow to stand 2–3 minutes.

SPINACH △
Cover and cook without water, stirring halfway through. Stand 3 minutes.

Microwave time on High in minutes

Fresh Vegetables		500 W oven	600 W oven	700 W oven
Broccoli	(1 cup/225 g)	5–6 mins	4–5 mins	3–4 mins
Brussels Sprouts	(1 cup/225 g)	5–6 mins	4–5 mins	3–4 mins
Cabbage	(1 cup/225 g)	3–5 mins	2–4 mins	2–4 mins
Cauliflower	(1 cup/225 g)	6–8 mins	4–6 mins	3–5 mins
	(2 cups/450 g)	10–12 mins	8–10 mins	6–8 mins
Spinach	(2 cups/225 g)	2–5 mins	2–4 mins	2–3 mins

45 SHOOTS & BULBS

Cut away roots and coarse parts of stems, and peel and slice as necessary. Stir or rearrange once or twice during cooking.

ARTICHOKE △
Cook in a covered dish or roasting bag with 4 tbsp (60 ml) water, and 2 tbsp (30 ml) lemon juice. Stand for 3–5 minutes.

◁ ASPARAGUS
Trim woody stems and arrange with tips in center. Sprinkle with 1 tbsp (15 ml) water, cover, and cook. When ready, thicker ends will be tender. Stand 3 minutes.

LEEKS △
Trim and cut into even slices. Add 2 tbsp (30 ml) water, cover, and cook. Stand 3–5 minutes.

◁ CELERY
Cut into ½ in (1 cm) slices. Add 4 tbsp (60 ml) water, cover, and cook. Stand 3 minutes.

ONIONS ▷
Cook sliced onions, covered, in 2 tbsp (30 ml) water, or in 1 tbsp (15 ml) warmed oil. Stand 3 minutes.

Microwave time on High in minutes

Fresh Vegetables		500 W oven	600 W oven	700 W oven
Artichoke	(1 large)	6–7 mins	5–6 mins	4–5 mins
	(2 large)	9–10 mins	.7–8 mins	6–7 mins
Asparagus	(½ bunch)	6–10 mins	5–8 mins	4–6 mins
Celery	(1 cup/225 g)	6–8 mins	5–7 mins	4–6 mins
Leeks	(2 cups/225 g)	3–6 mins	3–5 mins	2–4 mins
Onions	(1 medium)	4–6 mins	3–5 mins	2–4 mins

46 FRUIT VEGETABLES

These vegetables have moist flesh that absorbs flavors, so sprinkle with herbs and black pepper. During cooking, rearrange or stir once.

◁ BELL PEPPERS
Cut into rings, slices, or halves. Cover and cook in 1 tbsp (15 ml) water or hot oil. Stand 3–4 minutes.

◁ WINTER SQUASH
Cut in half, cover with waxed paper, and bake one half at a time. Stand 2 minutes, then scoop out seeds and purée flesh.

TOMATOES △
Slice or cut in half. Place in a covered dish and cook without water. Stand 2–3 minutes.

EGGPLANT △
Trim, pierce skin, and bake whole, wrapped in paper towels. Stew slices, covered, in 1 tbsp (15 ml) water or hot oil. Stand 4 minutes.

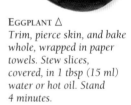

ZUCCHINI ▷
Cut into strips or rings, and allow to stew, covered, in their own juices. Stand 3 minutes.

Microwave time on High in minutes

Fresh Vegetables		500 W oven	600 W oven	700 W oven
Bell Peppers	(1 cup/225 g)	2–3 min	2–3 mins	1–2 mins
Eggplant	(½ medium)	3–6 mins	3–5 mins	2–4 mins
	(1 medium)	6–10 mins	5–8 mins	4–6 mins
Tomatoes	(2 medium)	3–6 mins	3–5 mins	2–4 mins
Winter Squash	(1 lb/450 g)	7–10 mins	6–8 mins	5–6 mins
Zucchini	(2 cups/225 g)	5–7 mins	4–6 mins	3–5 mins

47 PODS & SEEDS

Shell peas and fava beans, and trim green and runner beans. Spread the vegetables out and cook in a shallow dish.

◁ **GREEN BEANS**
Place in a dish, add 3 tbsp (45 ml) water, and cover. Stir once during the cooking time. Allow to stand 3 minutes.

◁ **SNOW PEAS**
Trim tops off the pods. Arrange in a dish with 2 tbsp (30 ml) water, cover, and cook. Stir once, and stand 3 minutes.

RUNNER BEANS ▷
String and slice beans, add 30 ml (2 tbsp) water, cover, and cook. Stir 2–3 times. Allow longer for larger beans.

PEAS △
Cook, covered, in 2 tbsp (30 ml) water. Stir during cooking. Leave to stand 3–5 minutes.

FAVA BEANS △
Cook, covered, with 3 tbsp (45 ml) water. Stir once. Stand 5 minutes.

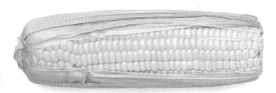

◁ **CORN ON THE COB**
Cover and cook in 1 tbsp (15 ml) water per cob, turning halfway through. Stand 2–3 minutes.

Microwave time on High in minutes

Fresh Vegetables		500 W oven	600 W oven	700 W oven
Corn on	(1 ear)	5–6 mins	4–5 mins	3–4 mins
the Cob	(2 ears)	8–10 mins	6–8 mins	5–7 mins
Fava Beans	(1 cup/225 g)	8–10 mins	6–8 mins	5–7 mins
Green Beans	(1½ cups/225 g)	6–9 mins	5–7 mins	4–6 mins
Peas	(2 cups/450 g)	6–8 mins	5–7 mins	4–6 mins
Runner Beans	(1½ cups/225 g)	6–8 mins	5–7 mins	4–6 mins
Snow Peas	(1½ cups/225 g)	7–9 mins	6–7 mins	5–6 mins

48 ROOTS & TUBERS

Cook potatoes and baby carrots and turnips whole. Make sure that vegetables, whether whole, sliced, or cubed, are of an even size, and arrange thinner parts in the center.

PARSNIPS ▷
Peel, then slice or dice. Cover and cook in 2 tbsp (30 ml) water and a few drops of lemon juice. Stir once. Stand 3 minutes.

RUTABAGA △
Peel and dice. Place in a dish with 2 tbsp (30 ml) water, cover, and cook, stirring once or twice. Stand 2 minutes.

◁ CARROTS
Leave baby carrots whole; slice larger ones. Add 3 tbsp (45 ml) water, cover, and cook. Stir once or twice. Allow to stand 3 minutes.

◁ TURNIPS
Peel and slice, but leave baby turnips whole. Cook, covered, in 2 tbsp (30 ml) water, stirring twice. Stand 3–5 minutes.

POTATOES △
Scrub, pierce skins, wrap in paper towels, and place in a circle. Rearrange halfway through cooking. Stand 5 minutes.

Microwave time on High in minutes

Fresh Vegetables		500 W oven	600 W oven	700 W oven
Carrots	(1 cup/225 g)	5–8 mins	4–6 mins	3–5 mins
Parsnips	(2 cups/450 g)	6–10 mins	5–8 mins	4–7 mins
Potatoes	(1 large)	5–6 mins	4–5 mins	3–4 mins
	(2 large)	10–15 mins	8–10 mins	6–8 mins
Rutabaga	(2 cups/450 g)	10–12 mins	8–10 mins	7–9 mins
Turnips	(2 cups/450 g)	10–12 mins	8–10 mins	6–8 mins

49 FRUIT

Peel, slice, and core larger fruits as necessary, and hull or trim berries. For a purée, cook the fruits for a few minutes more.

RHUBARB ▷
Sprinkle with grated orange peel or ginger, and cover. Stir twice. Stand 3 minutes.

◁ ▽ **BLACKCURRANTS & BLUEBERRIES**
Add 1 tbsp (15 ml) honey, if liked. Cover and cook, stirring once. Allow to stand 3 minutes.

△ **PEARS**
Cover cored halves and cook in 2 tbsp (30 ml) orange juice. Rearrange once. Stand 3 minutes.

△ **GOOSEBERRIES**
Cook, covered, with 1 tbsp (15 ml) honey. Stir once. Stand 3 minutes.

△ **BLACKBERRIES**
Hull and wash. Place in a dish without any liquid and cover. Stir once during cooking. Stand 3 minutes.

△ **APPLES**
Sprinkle slices with lemon juice and honey. Score cored whole apples around the center. Cover and cook, stirring slices during cooking. Stand 3 minutes.

Microwave time on High in minutes

Fresh Fruit		500 W oven	600 W oven	700 W oven
Apples	(1 cup/225 g)	3–5 mins	3–4 mins	2–3 mins
Blackberries	(2 cups/225 g)	2–5 mins	2–4 mins	2–3 mins
Blackcurrants	(2 cups/225 g)	2–5 mins	2–4 mins	2–3 mins
Blueberries	(2 cups/225 g)	2–5 mins	2–4 mins	2–3 mins
Gooseberries	(2 cups/225 g)	2–5 mins	2–4 mins	2–3 mins
Pears	(1 cup/225 g)	3–5 mins	3–4 mins	2–3 mins
Rhubarb	(2 cups/225 g)	5–7 mins	4–6 mins	3–5 mins

50 PEAS & BEANS

Presoak all dried peas and beans, except split peas and lentils, for 8 hours, rinse, and cook, allowing room for them to swell. Boil all larger peas and beans hard for the first 10 minutes.

GREEN PEAS

RED LENTILS

YELLOW PEAS

WHOLE BROWN LENTILS △
Sieve to remove grit, and rinse. Place in a large dish and cover with boiling water. Cook, covered, stirring 2 or 3 times. Stand 10–15 minutes.

SPLIT PEAS & LENTILS △ ▷
Place in a large dish and cover with boiling water. Stand on a plate in case the liquid boils over. Cover and cook, stirring once or twice. Stand 5–10 minutes.

BUTTER BEANS

RED KIDNEY BEANS

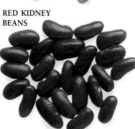

◁ △ LARGE BEANS
Put presoaked beans in a large dish. Pour over fresh boiling water. Cover and cook, making sure that the water is boiling hard for the first 10 minutes. Stir 2 or 3 times. Stand 5–10 minutes. If still hard, cook 5–10 minutes more.

CHICK PEAS △
In a large dish, pour boiling water over peas. Cook, covered, stirring 2 or 3 times. Stand 5–10 minutes.

Microwave time on High in minutes

Dried Peas & Beans		500 W oven	600 W oven	700 W oven
Chick Peas	1 cup (225 g)	20–30 mins	20–30 mins	20–30 mins
Butter Beans	1 cup (225 g)	20–30 mins	20–30 mins	20–30 mins
Red Kidney Beans	1 cup (225 g)	20–30 mins	20–30 mins	20–30 mins
Red Lentils	1 cup (225 g)	12–15 mins	10–12 mins	8–10 mins
Split Peas	1 cup (225 g)	12–15 mins	10–12 mins	8–10 mins
Whole Brown Lentils	1 cup (225 g)	15–20 mins	15–20 mins	15–20 mins

51 GRAINS & CEREALS

Grains cooked in the microwave stay separate and have a light, fluffy texture. Choose a large container to give them enough room to swell, and cover it loosely to let steam escape.

COUSCOUS ▽
Stir in 1¼ cups (300 ml) boiling water. Cover and cook, stirring once. Stand 5 minutes, drain, and toss.

BROWN RICE △
Place in a large container, and fill with double the quantity of boiling water. Cover and cook, stirring once halfway through. Stand 5–10 minutes.

BULGUR △
Place in a bowl, add 1¼ cups (300 ml) boiling water, and stir. Cover and cook, stirring once. Stand 5 minutes, then drain, fluff, and season.

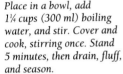

◁ OATMEAL
To make oatmeal for one, place in a serving bowl and stir in 2–3 times its volume in cold water or cold milk, Cook, covered. Stir once or twice during cooking. Stand 3 minutes, then stir.

BASMATI RICE △
In a large bowl, combine rice with 2 cups (400 ml) boiling water. Cover, cook, and stir 2 or 3 times during cooking. Stand 5 minutes. Drain if necessary.

Microwave time on High in minutes		500 W oven	600 W oven	700 W oven
Grains & Cereals				
Basmati Rice	(1 cup/225 g)	12–15 mins	12–15 mins	12–15 mins
Brown Rice	(1 cup/225 g)	16–20 mins	16–20 mins	16–20 mins
Bulgur	(½ cup/100 g)	2–3 mins	2–3 mins	2–3 mins
Couscous	(½ cup/100 g)	2–3 mins	2–3 mins	2–3 mins
Oatmeal	(½ cup/50 g)	4–6 mins	3–5 mins	2–4 mins

52 PASTA

Cooking pasta in the microwave isn't faster than the normal method, but it saves on messy saucepans. To prevent sticking, add 1 teaspoon of oil to the cooking water.

◁ **TAGLIATELLE**
Place in a bowl, cover completely with boiling water, and stir. Cook uncovered, stirring once. Stand 3 minutes.

PASTA TUBES ▷
Immerse pasta in boiling water. Stir, and cook uncovered. Stir once during cooking. Stand 3 minutes.

TUBE   TWIST

PASTA SHAPES ▷
Pour enough boiling water over pasta to cover it completely. Stir and cook uncovered, stirring once. Stand 3 minutes.

BOW

△ **LASAGNE (DRIED)**
Cover with boiling water. Cook without a cover, stirring once. Stand 5–10 minutes. Bake fresh and precooked lasagne in pasta dishes without prior cooking.

◁ **SPAGHETTI**
Place in a dish, and immerse in boiling water. Leave uncovered and cook, stirring once, then leave to stand 5 minutes.

Microwave time on High in minutes

		500 W oven	600 W oven	700 W oven
Dried Pasta				
Lasagne	(8 oz/225 g)	8–10 mins	8–10 mins	8–10 mins
Pasta Shapes	(8 oz/225 g)	6–8 mins	6–8 mins	6–8 mins
Pasta Tubes	(8 oz/225 g)	6–8 mins	6–8 mins	6–8 mins
Spaghetti	(8 oz/225 g)	6–8 mins	6–8 mins	6–8 mins
Tagliatelle	(8 oz/225 g)	2–5 mins	2–4 mins	2–4 mins

53 FLAT FISH

These fish are very thin and cook so fast that you don't always need to turn them during cooking.

- **Dover Sole** This has an excellent flavor and firm texture. Cook fillets like lemon sole. Skin and remove head of whole fish, then bake with butter, lemon juice, and herbs.
- **Halibut** You can buy halibut in fillets. It has soft, white flesh. Bake the fillets like flounder, or cook with olive oil in a browning dish.

◁ SKATE (WINGS)
Choose wings that weigh 8 oz (225 g) each. Preheat a browning dish for 5 minutes, add 2 tbsp (25 g) butter, and cook 2 wings at a time. Turn over halfway through. Stand 3 minutes.

LEMON SOLE △
On the skinned side of fillets, spread a stuffing made from fresh bread crumbs, mushrooms, butter, and minced fish. Roll up. Place on a greased dish with white wine, cover, and cook. Stand 3 minutes.

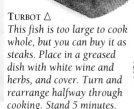

TURBOT △
This fish is too large to cook whole, but you can buy it as steaks. Place in a greased dish with white wine and herbs, and cover. Turn and rearrange halfway through cooking. Stand 5 minutes.

◁ FLOUNDER
Cook whole or as fillets. Place in a greased dish with butter and lemon juice, and cover. Stand 3 minutes.

Microwave time on High in minutes

Fresh Fish		500 W oven	600 W oven	700 W oven
Dover Sole	(1 lb/450 g)	5–7 mins	4–6 mins	3–4 mins
Flounder	(1 lb/450 g)	5–7 mins	4–6 mins	3–4 mins
Halibut	(8 oz/225 g)	5–6 mins	3–4 mins	2–3 mins
	(1 lb/450 g)	8–9 mins	5–6 mins	4–5 mins
Lemon Sole	(8 oz/225 g)	5–6 mins	3–4 mins	2–3 mins
Skate	(1 lb/450 g)	4–5 mins	3½–4 mins	2½–3 mins
Turbot	(1 lb/450 g)	5–7 mins	4–6 mins	3–4 mins

54 ROUND FISH

If you are cooking a whole round fish, score it on both sides to prevent overcooking. Round fish need to be gutted before cooking.

- **Cod** Sold as steaks, this fish has firm, white flesh. Cook the steaks covered, turning halfway through cooking, and stand 3 minutes.

- **Haddock** This has very firm flesh. Cook fresh fillets like cod – covered, turning halfway through the cooking time. Let stand 3 minutes.

- **Herring** Cook this tasty, oily fish in a browning dish, preheated for 5 minutes, with butter. Turn it once, cover, and stand 3 minutes.

◁ MACKEREL
Choose very fresh mackerel. Place in a greased dish with 2 tbsp (30 ml) water. Cover the dish and cook, turning after half the cooking time. Stand 5 minutes. Serve with cranberry or rhubarb sauce.

SARDINE (FRESH) ▷
Preheat a browning dish for 5 minutes. Add 2 tbsp (30 ml) olive oil, then the scored and gutted sardines, and cover. Turn over one-third of the way through cooking. Stand 3 minutes.

◁ SEA BASS
Grease a dish with butter and add fish. Brush fish, inside and outside, with melted butter. Cover and cook, turning fish or rotating dish halfway through cooking. Stand 5 minutes.

TROUT ▷
Rainbow and other varieties of trout are now farmed and widely available. Score, place in a buttered dish with lemon juice, cover, and cook. Turn halfway through, adding 2 oz (50 g) flaked almonds. Stand 5 minutes.

SALMON △
Cook whole fish, covered, with 5 tbsp
(75 ml) each water and white wine,
peppercorns, and herbs. Stand 5 minutes.
Wrap steaks in waxed paper and cook,
turning once. Stand 3 minutes.

WHITING ▽
This fish is normally sold as fillets, and
has flaky, flavorful flesh. Cook in a dish,
overlapping the thin ends, with 2–3 tbsp
(30–45 ml) white wine and
some herbs. Cover, turn
once during cooking, and
let stand 5 minutes.

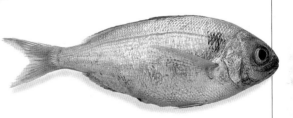

PORGY OR RED BREAM ▷
Score whole fish and place in
a dish with 5 tbsp (30–45 ml)
each olive oil and lemon juice,
and chopped chives. Marinate
for 30 minutes. Cook, covered.
Turn once during cooking.

Microwave time on High in minutes

Fresh Fish		500 W oven	600 W oven	700 W oven
Cod	(8 oz/225 g)	5–6 mins	3–4 mins	2–3 mins
Haddock	(8 oz/225 g)	5–6 mins	3–4 mins	2–3 mins
Herring	(2 x 6 oz/175 g)	7–9 mins	5–6 mins	4–5 mins
Mackerel	(2 x 1 lb/450 g)	18–19 mins	16–17 mins	14–15 mins
Porgy	(1 lb/450 g)	5–7 mins	4–6 mins	3–4 mins
Salmon	(1 lb/450 g)	5–7 mins	4–6 mins	3–4 mins
Salmon Steaks	(8 oz/225 g)	5–6 mins	3–4 mins	2–3 mins
Sardines, fresh	(4 x 3 oz/75 g)	8–10 mins	6–7 mins	5–6 mins
Sea Bass	(1 x 3.3 lb/1.4 kg)	8–9 mins	7–8 mins	6–7 mins
Trout	(2 x 8 oz/225 g)	10–12 mins	6–8 mins	5–6 mins
Whiting	(8 oz/225 g)	5–6 mins	3–4 mins	2–3 mins

55 SHELLFISH & SEAFOOD

Cook large shellfish, such as lobster or crab, conventionally. Smaller shellfish, such as mussels, microwave very successfully, but you will need to watch the timings carefully because these shellfish lose moisture easily.

CLAMS △
Use large clams for chowder, or cook them like mussels. Prepare smaller clams by washing and placing in a large bowl. Cover and cook, stirring often. Stand 3 minutes. Remove top shells, and serve with garlic butter.

◁ SEA SCALLOPS
Slice flesh and cook, covered, with lemon juice and herbs. Stir during cooking. Let stand 3 minutes.

MUSSELS ▷
Cook on the day you buy them. Wash, scrape the shells clean, and pull off the beards. Discard broken mussels, or any that don't close when tapped. Place in a bowl with some white wine, cover, and cook. Stand 3 minutes. Discard closed mussels.

◁ SQUID
Fill prepared squid with bread crumb, sautéed onion, and herb stuffing. Close the ends with toothpicks. Poach, covered, in 1¼ cups (300 ml) fresh tomato sauce. Stir occasionally. Let stand 3 minutes.

CRAYFISH ▷
This freshwater shellfish
is really a tiny lobster,
and is small enough to
be cooked in the
microwave. It
is sold raw or
cooked, with
or without its
head. To heat
or cook crayfish,
place in a dish, and
cover. Stand 3 minutes.

▷ LANGOUSTINES,
SMALL LOBSTERS, OR
LARGE CRAYFISH
You must kill these
shellfish before cooking
them in the microwave.
To heat or cook them, place
them in a covered dish. At
the end of the cooking time,
let stand 3 minutes.

SHRIMP △
Place raw shrimp in a bowl, cover, and
cook, tossing two or three times
during cooking until they change
color. Stand 3 minutes. Heat cooked
shrimp, covered, on a plate with
garlic butter and herbs, if liked.

Microwave time on High in minutes

Fresh Shellfish		500 W oven	600 W oven	700 W oven
Clams	(1½ lb/675 g)	5–7 mins	4–6 mins	3–4 mins
Crayfish	(8 oz/225 g)	1–1½ mins	¾–1 min	½–¾ min
Mussels	(1½ lb/675 g)	5–7 mins	4–6 mins	3–4 mins
Sea Scallops	(12 large)	14–16 mins	12–14 mins	10–12 mins
Shrimp	(1 lb/450 g)	3–6 mins	2–4 mins	1–3 mins
Langoustines, Small Lobsters, or Large Crayfish	(8 oz/225 g)	1–1½ mins	¾–1 min	½–¾ mins
Squid	(1 lb/450 g)	9–11 mins	8–10 mins	6–7 mins

56 BEEF

Properly cooked microwaved beef is tender and moist. Test with a meat thermometer: 120° F (50° C) for rare; 135° F (57° C) for medium; 150° F (66° C) for well-done.

- **Ground Beef** Place beef in a bowl, and cook on High. Stir two or three times during cooking. Add any sauce ingredients, vegetables, or herbs halfway through the cooking time. Cook 5 minutes more, or until the vegetables are tender.
- **Hamburgers** Arrange on a greased dish, and cook on High. Turn over halfway through cooking, rearrange, and drain off the juices.
- **Round** Place the meat in a large bowl. Add ½ cup (110 ml) water, 3 tsp tomato purée, a bouquet garni, and 1 tbsp gravy granules. Cover, and cook on High for 6–8 minutes, then Medium. Stir the sauce during cooking. Let stand 20 minutes.
- **Sirloin** Heat a browning dish on High for 5 minutes. Add 2 tsp oil,

BURGERS IN BUNS

then the steak, and press down well. Turn a third of the way through cooking. Stand 4 minutes.

- **Stew Meat** Blade bone and chuck are sold for braising and for making stews. Cube the meat, and place in a bowl with sliced onions. Cover and cook on High for 5 minutes, then stir in ¼ cup (25 g) flour, 1¼ cups (300 ml) boiling stock and herbs. Cook on High for 5 minutes more, then Medium, stirring during cooking. Stand 10 minutes.

Microwave time on High in minutes

Fresh Beef		500 W oven	600 W oven	700 W oven
Ground Beef	(8 oz/225 g)	9–10 mins	6 mins	3 mins
Hamburgers	(4 oz/100 g)	5½–6 mins	4 mins	3 mins
	(8 oz/225 g)	9 mins	6 mins	5 mins
Sirloin	(2 x 1 lb/450 g)			
	rare	4 mins	2½–3 mins	2–2½ mins
	medium	6½ mins	5 mins	3½ mins
	well-done	8–9 mins	7–7½ mins	4½–5 mins
Round	(3 lb/1.4 kg)	55–60 mins	50–55 mins	45–50 mins
Stew Meat	(1 lb/450 g)	60–65 mins	55–60 mins	50–55 mins

57 LAMB

Roast larger cuts, flavored with rosemary and garlic. Cook cheaper cuts slowly, in stews.

- **Leg** Wrap the bony end with foil, and cook on a roasting rack above a dish. Remove foil, and turn halfway through cooking. Stand 15 minutes. You can also use this cut for kebabs.
- **Loin Chops** Spread in a single layer in a dish. Turn and rearrange halfway through. Stand 5 minutes.
- **Neck Slices** Heat a browning dish for 5 minutes. Add 2 tsp oil, then the cutlets, and press down. Turn a third of the way through the cooking time. Stand 3 minutes.
- **Shoulder** Place on a rack above a dish, inserting slivers of garlic and rosemary leaves into the fat to add

BONED LOIN CHOP WITH VEGETABLES

flavor. Roast, turning after half the cooking time. Stand 15 minutes. Also casserole (*see Stew Meat*).

- **Stew Meat** Use in Irish Stew. Layer with 1½ lb (675 g) sliced potatoes, 2 sliced onions, and 1 cup (250 ml) water. Cover and cook on High for 5 minutes, then reduce to Low. Let stand 10 minutes.

Microwave time on High in minutes

Fresh Lamb		500 W oven	600 W oven	700 W oven
Leg, with bone	(1 lb/450 g)			
	med-rare	12–13 mins	9 mins	8 mins
	well-done	15 mins	10 mins	7 mins
	kebabs	10–13 mins	7–10 mins	5–7 mins
Loin Chops	(1 lb/450 g)			
	med-rare	10 mins	7 mins	5 mins
	well-done	13 mins	10 mins	7 mins
Neck Slices	(4 x 3 oz/85 g)			
	med-rare	7 mins	5 mins	4 mins
	well-done	8 mins	6 mins	5 mins
Shoulder, rolled	(1 lb/450 g)			
	med-rare	14 mins	10 mins	8 mins
	well-done	16–17 mins	12 mins	9 mins
	cubed	55–60 mins	35–40 mins	30–35 mins
Stew Meat	(1½ lb/675 g)	80–85 mins	70–75 mins	60–65 mins

58 PORK

If not thoroughly cooked, pork can be dangerous. Check that the meat is not pink in the center, and test it with a meat thermometer before leaving it to stand: it should read 165° F (74° C), rising to 170° F (80° C) on standing. To keep chops, bacon, and ham steaks from curling, snip fat every ¾ in (2 cm).

■ **Bacon** Place on a rack and dish, cover with paper towels to prevent fat splatters, and cook. Turn halfway through and remove paper. Serve regular slices at once; let Canadian bacon stand 3 minutes.

■ **Leg** Check that the rind is deeply scored, and rub it with salt and oil, to make good crackling. Place on a roasting rack and dish, with the fat side down, shielding the bone ends with foil. Turn halfway through the cooking time. Stand 15–20 minutes.

■ **Loin Chops** Arrange on a dish, and cook, turning over after half the cooking time. Stand 5 minutes.

PORK WITH VEGETABLES

■ **Spare Ribs** Place in a dish with ¼ cup (100 ml) water. Cover, and cook on High for 5 minutes, then reduce to Medium. Halfway through cooking, drain off fat, turn over, and brush with barbecue or sweet and sour sauce. Stand 5 minutes.

■ **Sausages** Pierce skins, and place in a dish, brushing with browning agent, if you wish. Cover and cook, turning and rearranging sausages two or three times. Stand 3 minutes.

Microwave time on High in minutes

Fresh Pork & Pork Products		500 W oven	600 W oven	700 W oven
Bacon Slices	(4)	3 mins	3 mins	2 mins
Canadian Bacon	(2 x 3 oz/85 g)	6–8 mins	4–5 mins	3–4 mins
Leg of Pork	(1 lb/450 g)			
	with bone	12–14 mins	10–12 mins	8–9 mins
	boned	14–15 mins	11–13 mins	9–10 mins
Loin Chops	(2 x 6 oz/180 g)	5–6 mins	4–5 mins	3–4 mins
Sausages	(8 oz/225 g)	8 mins	6 mins	4 mins
	(1 lb/450 g)	12 mins	8 mins	6 mins
Spare Ribs	(1 lb/450 g)	11–13 mins	10–11 mins	8–10 mins

59 POULTRY

Place whole birds on a roasting rack so that the fat can drain off. To promote browning, insert both the bird and rack inside a roasting bag. Cover larger birds with a slit bag.

Chicken Place on a roasting rack inside a pierced roasting bag. Turn over after half the cooking time. Let the bird stand 10–15 minutes.

Chicken Parts Spread out in a single layer, with the thinner ends towards the center, and brush with barbecue or soy sauce. Turn or rearrange pieces halfway through the cooking time. Stand 5 minutes.

■ **Duck** Prick all over, and rub skin with salt for crispness and flavor. Place, breast side down, on a rack over a deep dish, and cook. Drain off juices halfway through cooking, and turn over. Stand 15 minutes.

■ **Turkey** Place on a roasting rack over a dish, resting the bird on one side of the breast. Cook, turning

CLASSIC ROAST CHICKEN

onto the other side of the breast a third of the way through cooking, and on to its back in the final third. Shield any parts that are in danger of overcooking with foil. Let the turkey stand 20 minutes.

■ **Turkey Parts** These include cuts such as whole breasts, as well as whole boneless rolls. Place on a roasting rack and dish, with the meat side down if the parts you are cooking include the bone. Shield bony parts with foil. Cook, remove the foil halfway through, and turn.

Microwave time on High in minutes

Fresh Poultry		500 W oven	600 W oven	700 W oven
Chicken	(3 lb/1.4 kg)	26–28 mins	18–20 mins	14–16 mins
Chicken Parts	(3 oz/2 x 75 g)	5 mins	4 mins	3 mins
	(2 x 8 oz/225 g)	12 mins	8 mins	6 mins
Duck	(4 lb/1.75 kg)	38–40 mins	26–30 mins	20–24 mins
Turkey	(6 lb/2.75 kg)	60–75 mins	40–55 mins	30–40 mins
Turkey Parts	(1 lb/450 g)	10–12 mins	8–10 mins	6–7 mins
	(2 lb/900 g)	16–20 mins	13–15 mins	9–12 mins

60 VEAL

Take care not to overcook veal, as it dries out easily. Marinate roasts to tenderize and flavor them.

- **Scallops** Heat a browning dish for 5 minutes. Add 2 tsp oil, 1 tbsp (15 g) butter, and finally the veal slices, pressing them down. Cook on High for 1 minute on both sides, then Medium. Stand 2 minutes.

- **Loin** Place on a rack and dish, fat side down, inside a pierced roasting bag. Turn over halfway through the cooking time. Stand 5 minutes.
- **Loin Chops** Heat a browning dish for 5 minutes, add 2 tsp oil, and then the chops. Press them down, turning over after a third of the cooking time. Stand 5 minutes.

Microwave time on High in minutes

Fresh Veal		500 W oven	600 W oven	700 W oven
Loin	(1 lb/450 g) with bone	12–14 mins	10–12 mins	8–9 mins
	boned & rolled	12–15 mins	10–13 mins	8–10 mins
Loin Chops	(2 x 8 oz/225 g)	7 mins	6 mins	5 mins
Scallops	(2 x 4 oz/110 g)	7 mins	6 mins	5 mins

61 ORGAN MEATS

Liver and kidney toughen if at all overcooked, so cook carefully.

- **Kidney** Use calf's and ox's kidneys only in stews. Halve lamb's and chop pig's kidneys, after removing the outer membrane, then snip out the white core. Heat a browning dish for 5 minutes, then cook the kidneys with a little oil, pressing down and turning once. Stand 3 minutes.

- **Liver** Peel skin and cut away any tough membranes. Soak pig's and ox's liver in milk for a few hours, and leave whole, but slice calf's and lamb's liver. Cook with a little oil in a browning dish preheated for 5 minutes, turning one-third of the way through cooking. Cook pig's and ox's liver in stock for 25–30 minutes more. Stand 5 minutes.

Microwave time on High in minutes

Fresh Organ Meats		500 W oven	600W oven	700W oven
Kidney	(8 oz/225 g)	9–10 mins	7–8 mins	5–6 mins
	(1 lb/450 g)	13–14 mins	11–12 mins	8–9 mins
Liver	(8 oz/225 g)	6–7 mins	4–5 mins	3–4 mins
	(1 lb/450 g)	10–11 mins	7–8 mins	5–6 mins
	pig & ox liver	+ 25–30 mins	+ 25–30 mins	+ 25–30 mins

TIMESAVING TECHNIQUES

62 COMBINED TECHNIQUES

Use your microwave in combination with conventional cooking techniques to save time, and for convenience.

- Boil pasta on the stove, leaving your microwave free to cook the sauce at the same time.
- Place a microwaved casserole under the broiler to brown while you cook the vegetables in the microwave.
- Cut barbecuing time in half by partially cooking meat and poultry in the microwave, then finishing it off on the barbecue. Be sure to transfer it immediately, though, as harmful bacteria can grow in food left out at room temperature.

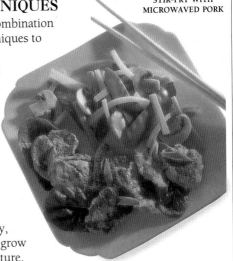

STIR-FRY WITH MICROWAVED PORK

TOMATOES WITH SPLIT SKINS

63 PEEL TOMATOES

Pour 2½ cups (600 ml) boiling water into a microwave-safe container, and add 2 tomatoes. Heat on High for 45–60 seconds, or until the skins have split. Remove the tomatoes, plunge briefly into cold water, and then drain. Now you should be able to peel off the skins without any difficulty.

64 PEEL ONIONS & GARLIC

Place two small, trimmed onions in a microwave-safe bowl. Heat on High for 45 seconds, then squeeze the onions at the stalk end until they pop out of their skins.

To peel garlic, place 3 cloves on the oven floor. Heat on High for 15–30 seconds, until the cloves are just warm. Squeeze them at one end until they slide out of their skin.

SQUEEZE OFF WARMED GARLIC SKINS

65 POULTRY TIPS

If you are cooking poultry pieces in a sauce, skin them first to allow the sauce to penetrate right through to the flesh.

- Place a loose covering of waxed paper over crumb-coated poultry to keep the coating from becoming soggy.
- If you are cooking a bird with stuffing, leave it in the microwave for 5 minutes longer than you would an unstuffed bird.
- Pierce duck skin to allow the fat to drain, and to keep the skin from splitting.

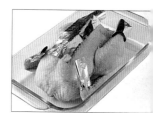

△ **PREVENT OVERCOOKING**
Protect chicken breastbone and wing and leg tips with foil.

△ **SLOW COOKERS**
Duck legs take longer to cook than breasts. Serve with sauce.

◁ **MORE HEALTHY**
Remove fatty poultry skin, and coat portions with melted butter or margarine and crumbs.

66 MEAT TIPS

Areas of fat attract microwave energy and cause uneven cooking, so trim excess fat off meat before cooking.

- To remove excess fat from ground meat, place the meat in a colander over a bowl and heat it on High so that the fat melts. Allow 4 minutes per 1 lb (450 g) ground meat, and stir twice.
- For tender roast meat, sprinkle it with water and rub on meat tenderizer.

TENDERIZE MEAT FOR ROASTING
Rub on tenderizer, then pierce the meat to allow tenderizer to soak in.

67 CITRUS TIPS

Peeling and squeezing juice from citrus fruit is easier if you warm the fruit in the microwave, but always prick the skin in several places first. Set the oven to High and microwave the citrus fruit for 15–20 seconds.

- To dry pieces of peel, scrub well, spread on paper towels, and heat on High for 1 minute. Rearrange once.
- Dry grated peel in a bowl, heated on High for 30–60 seconds, stirring once.

MORE JUICE
Place fruit on the oven floor. Heat on High for 30 seconds, then squeeze.

68 HOW TO COOK BEANS

Presoak beans and cook them in the normal amount of water, but place them in a larger-than-usual container to allow them to swell and to prevent the rapidly boiling water from spilling over the edge. To guard against possible food poisoning, boil red kidney beans rapidly for 10 minutes first on a conventional stove.

MIXED BEAN SALAD

69 HOW TO STEAM VEGETABLES

Place vegetables in a bowl with 30–45 ml (2–3 tbsp) water, and they will cook in the steam produced by the water. Steaming is a particularly healthy way of cooking vegetables; so little water is used that fewer of their soluble nutrients are lost.

NEAPOLITAN BROCCOLI
Cook broccoli with olives, red peppers, capers, garlic, and almonds.

70 COOKING TIMES

If you want to convert one of your favorite conventional recipes, use a microwave recipe with similar ingredients and quantities as your model, and remember the following:
- As a general guide, cut the normal cooking time by at least half.
- Foods will continue to cook after being removed from the oven, so take this into account. The thicker or denser the food, the longer the cooking and standing times.

SMALLER PIECES COOK FASTER

71 REDUCE LIQUID

You should generally reduce the amount of liquid required in a conventional recipe by a quarter or a third when cooking it in the microwave. Watch the food during the cooking period; if it begins to look too dry, you can always add more liquid.

LESS LIQUID

58

72 WHEN TO SEASON

Avoid adding salt to food before you cook it because salt has a dehydrating effect. Add to taste before serving.

You might like to add more herbs and spices to some dishes than you would when cooking them conventionally: microwave cooking is so quick that flavors don't have time to permeate foods in the same way.

WHOLE NUTMEG

GROUND NUTMEG

73 PREVENT FISH ODORS

Some fish have a strong odor that often lingers after cooking. To remove such odors, squeeze out some lemon juice and pour into a microwave-safe cup with some water. Place in the oven and allow the lemon juice and water mixture to boil for 3–4 minutes. Cooking with wine, vinegar, or lemon juice also helps minimize food odors, as well as giving flavor to the dish.

LEMONS

74 REHEATING BEANS, GRAINS, & PASTA

Leftovers or small portions of beans, grains, and pasta become dry if reheated conventionally. With a microwave oven, you can reheat these foods so that they retain all their texture and flavor.

- Place enough beans, grains, or pasta for one or two servings in a dish, toss in a little oil, and heat on High for 1–2 minutes.
- Cooking bean dishes in advance and then reheating them actually improves them as it gives their flavors time to develop fully.

GARDEN VEGETABLE & PASTA SALAD

75 TIME YOUR EGGS

You cannot boil eggs in their shells in the microwave, but you can scramble, bake, or poach them. Always pay special attention when cooking eggs because the timings will vary depending on the size, composition, and freshness of the eggs. It is best to take eggs out of the oven while they are still slightly undercooked; they can then finish cooking during the standing time.

POACHED EGGS

76 TAKE THE CHILL OFF CHEESE

If you keep your cheese in the refrigerator, you should bring it to room temperature before serving, to enjoy its full flavor. To take the chill off a 8 oz (225 g) piece of cheese, place the cheese on a microwave-safe plate, having removed any wrappings first. Just before it is time to serve the cheese, heat it on Medium for 45–60 seconds. Transfer the cheese to a cheese board, or serve on the dish on which you heated it.

CHEESE BOARD

77 TAKE THE CHILL OFF WINE

Red wines are generally best served at room temperature – only then can their flavor develop fully. If you do not have time to wait for wine to reach the right temperature, try this quick tip. Pour the wine out of the bottle into a microwave-safe pitcher, and heat it on High for 10 seconds. The wine should not be noticeably warm when you serve it, but should have a mellow smoothness.

RED WINE

78 WARM & SOFTEN FRUIT

APPLES

To take the chill off fruit that has been stored in the refrigerator, and to bring out its flavor, place it on a microwave-safe plate and heat it on High for 1–2 minutes.

To soften dried fruit, place 4 oz (110 g) fruit and ¼ cup (50 ml) water in a 1-quart (1-liter) measuring cup. Cover and heat on High for 45 seconds. Stand for 1 minute.

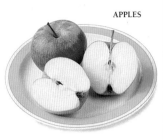

MELTED CHOCOLATE

79 HOW TO MELT CHOCOLATE

Chocolate burns if it becomes too hot, so melting it on a conventional burner can be tricky. To melt chocolate in the microwave, break it into pieces, and place 1 oz (25 g) in a microwave-safe bowl. Heat on High for 1–2 minutes, until the chocolate is soft and the surface is slightly shiny. Remove from the oven, and stir until the chocolate is melted, smooth, and lump-free.

80 BUTTER TIPS

Soften or melt butter to make it easier to spread, and for use in baking and frying.

- To soften butter, wrap half a stick (4 oz/110 g) in waxed paper. Place on a plate, and heat on Medium-Low for 30 seconds.
- Clarified butter does not burn easily, so it is ideal for frying. To clarify butter, cut it into cubes, and place half a stick (4 oz/110 g) in a 2-cup (500-ml) microwave-safe measuring cup. Heat on High for 1½–2 minutes, or until the butter has melted. Skim the foam off the top.

Remove foam from clarified butter

PYREX®

81 SOFTEN ICE CREAM

If ice cream is rock-hard when you take it from the freezer, soften it a little to make it easier to serve. To soften a 1-pint (500-ml) container of ice cream, set the oven to Medium-Low and place the container on the oven floor. Heat the ice cream for 15–20 seconds, until it has slightly softened (but do not allow it to melt).

SOFT ENOUGH TO SCOOP

REMOVE APPLE FROM SOFT SUGAR

82 SOFTEN BROWN SUGAR

Brown sugar can crystallize into solid lumps that are extremely difficult to break up. Soften the hardened sugar by placing it in a microwave-safe glass dish with an apple wedge or a slice of white bread. Cover the dish and place it in the microwave, then heat on High for 30–40 seconds. Allow the sugar to stand for 30 seconds more, then remove the apple wedge or the bread slice. Stir the sugar once to break it up.

83 SOFTEN HONEY

Honey may crystallize into granules and solidify if it is allowed to become too cold. To soften and make it runny again, remove the lid of the jar. Place the jar in the oven, and heat on High for 30 seconds. Stir until the honey loses its grainy texture and becomes smooth. If the honey is still grainy after you have warmed it, return the jar to the oven and heat once again.

RUNNY HONEY

84 SAUCE KNOW-HOW

If you want your sauces to be smooth, you must watch them carefully: they can thicken suddenly.

- Bring starch-thickened sauces to the boil and remove from the oven as soon as they have thickened. Do not overcook these sauces, or you will destroy the thickening agent and the sauce will start to separate.
- Save on cleanup by making a sauce in the same bowl in which you wish to serve it. Make sure that the bowl is large enough to allow for the sauce to bubble and to expand.

WHISK SMOOTH
If a sauce begins to thicken around the edges, whisk briskly to prevent lumps.

85 SHELL NUTS

Place 1 cup (140 g) nuts with ¼ cup (50 ml) water in a medium-size, microwave-safe bowl. Cover and heat on High for 2–3 minutes, or until the water is boiling. Remove the bowl from the oven, and leave to stand for 1 minute. Drain the water and shell the nuts.

SHELL WALNUTS

86 TOAST NUTS

The microwave cannot brown certain foods, but you can use it for toasting nuts. Shell the nuts first, if necessary, and spread ½ cup (50 g) out in a shallow, microwave-safe pie dish. Heat the nuts on High for 2½–4 minutes, stirring occasionally, until they are a light golden brown.

STIR NUTS FOR EVEN BROWNING

87 BLANCH ALMONDS

Pour 1¼ cups (300 ml) water into a 1-quart (1-liter) microwave-safe bowl, and heat it on High for 3–4 minutes. Add 1 cup (140 g) whole, shelled almonds to the water, and heat them on High for 1 minute. Drain off the water and let the nuts cool. The skins should now slip off easily when you squeeze them. Pat the almonds dry.

SQUEEZE OFF SKINS

88 TOAST SEEDS

Bring out the nutty flavor of seeds by toasting them in the microwave. Spread ½ cup (85 g) seeds out over the base of a shallow, microwave-safe pie dish. Heat them on High for 3–5 minutes, until they are golden. Stir to bring seeds from the edge to the center of the dish, so that they all receive the same amount of microwave energy.

STIR FOR EVEN TOASTING

89 HOW TO KEEP PASTRY CRISP

Baking pastry "blind" – without a filling – helps to keep it crisp. Line an 8-in (20-cm) pie dish with pastry, and prick the sides and base with a fork. Cover the pastry with a paper towel, to absorb moisture, and a plate, to keep the pastry from rising. Bake on High for 4–6 minutes. Leave to cool, uncovered, then fill. If you prefer, line the pastry case with waxed paper and dried beans before baking it.

FILL WITH DRIED BEANS

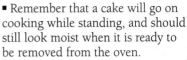

90 CAKE-BAKING

The same general guidelines apply to microwave cake-baking as to baking the conventional way, with a few important exceptions:
- Unless you use a bundt pan, the inside diameter of a cake container should not exceed 8 in (20 cm), or the center may not cook through.

- Remember that a cake will go on cooking while standing, and should still look moist when it is ready to be removed from the oven.
- Tap the sides of the container during the standing time to loosen the cake.

HEAT THE CENTER
Use a bundt pan for larger cakes. This will allow heat to reach the center more easily.

ALLOW ENOUGH SPACE
Half fill the container to allow the mixture to rise during cooking without overflowing.

91 JAM-MAKING

The microwave is ideal for making up a jar or two of jam or other preserves when fruit is plentiful.
- Sterilize jars for jam by half filling with water and heating them in the microwave until the water reaches boiling point. Swirl the water around the inside of each jar, then drain it off, and dry the jar well before filling.
- Jam mixtures will bubble up during cooking, so cook them in containers two or three times larger than the volume of jam being made.

MAKE SMALL QUANTITIES

92 MAKING DOUGH

Take some of the waiting out of bread-making by allowing the dough to prove in the microwave. Place the dough in the oven in a microwave-safe bowl with a 1-quart (1-liter) measuring cup containing 2½ cups (600 ml) of very hot water. Cover dough, and heat on Low for 20–25 minutes, until risen.

COVER DOUGH WITH PAPER TOWELS

93 WARM YOUR BREAD

Heat rolls and bread on High for 1–2 minutes just before serving. To save time, you can even heat breads in their serving basket.

- Freshen slightly stale bread by heating it on High for 15 seconds.
- Soften a large, unsliced, frozen loaf on Defrost for 7–9 minutes in a 600 W oven (5–7 minutes in a 700 W oven; 10–14 minutes in a 500 W oven). Stand 5–10 minutes.
- You can defrost a single slice of bread in just 10–15 seconds. Place the slice on a paper towel.

HOT CRUSTY ROLLS

94 HOW TO MAKE BREAD CRUMBS

If you have some slightly stale bread, do not throw it away, but use it to make dry bread crumbs for coating foods. Place a slice of bread in the oven, and heat on High for 2–3 minutes. Then place the bread in a bag and crush with a rolling pin, or reduce it to crumbs in a blender. Store the crumbs in an airtight container, ready for use when necessary.

CRUSH TOASTED BREAD

95 REFRESH POTATO CHIPS

If potato chips have become a little soggy, there's no need to throw them away – crisp them up again in the microwave. Lay a piece of paper towel on a microwave-safe plate; then, on top, arrange 1 cup (about 2 oz/50 g) potato chips in a shallow layer. Heat the chips on High for 15–60 seconds. Allow to stand for 5 minutes. The chips should now have regained all their crunchiness.

HEAT POTATO CHIPS

96 HOW TO DRY HERBS

When fresh herbs are available, dry small quantities – only about ¼ cup (15 g) at a time – for use all year round. The moisture content in such a small quantity of herbs is very low, so place a bowl of water in the oven with them to keep the paper towels from scorching. Watch the herbs carefully while drying, and rearrange several times. Let cool, before crushing through a sieve.

PARSLEY

SAGE

BASIL

1 Remove stalks from any leafy herbs. Rinse the herbs carefully, then pat dry with absorbent paper towels.

2 Spread the herbs out between two paper towels, and place in the oven. Add a small bowl of water for safety.

3 Heat the herbs on High for 4–6 minutes, until they lose their fresh color and become brittle. Crush and store in airtight jars.

97 HOW TO SOFTEN JAM

To scrape the last of the contents out of a jar of jam or other preserves, remove the lid and place the jar in the microwave on Defrost for 30 seconds. If jam has become thick and difficult to spread, you can also use your microwave to soften it. Remove the lid, then heat the jar on High for 1½–2 minutes per cup (225 g) jam, until the jam spreads easily.

SCRAPE OUT SOFT JAM

98 HEATING BABY FOOD

Using your microwave to heat bottled baby food in glass jars is much quicker and easier than the traditional method, in which the jar is left to stand in hot water. To warm a jar of baby food, remove the lid, place the jar in the oven, and heat on Medium for 40–60 seconds. Always stir baby food, then test the temperature before giving the food to your child: it should be just warm.

BABY FOOD

99 FREEZER TIPS

If you have a microwave, you will be able to defrost food from your freezer in just a matter of minutes.

- Defrost and cook frozen vegetables in one operation. Simply cook them in their freezer bag, piercing the bag first and resting it on a plate.
- Freeze foods in individual portions for faster defrosting.
- The flavor of seasonings can diminish in freezing, so check the seasoning when you reheat frozen food.

KEEP CENTER CLEAR
Place a paper cup or glass in the center when freezing a casserole. Defrosting will be quicker because food isn't concentrated in the middle.

100 ADVANCE COOKING FOR FLAVOR

Microwave cooking is so fast that the flavors in some dishes don't have time to develop fully and to blend with one another. If you are making a bean dish, or one-dish casserole, cook it in advance, and then reheat it for serving later. The "resting" time not only allows the flavors to mature, but the food will only need reheating to make it ready to serve.

FLAVORFUL COQ AU VIN

101 ADVANCE PRESENTATION

To avoid a last-minute rush, arrange individual portions on plates ahead of time, and then reheat them just before serving. An average-sized oven can take as many as three plates at a time. Place them on top of each other, on stacking rings made specially for microwave use. Alternatively, improvise and cover each plate with another upturned one or a large soup bowl, and place the next plate on top. Give the plates a half-turn every few minutes. The food is reheated when the bottoms of the plates feel warm.

THAI-STYLE STIR-FRY

INDEX

ACKNOWLEDGMENTS

Dorling Kindersley would like to thank Hilary Bird for compiling the index, Ann Kay for proofreading, Bella Pringle for editorial assistance, Murdo Culver for design assistance, Mark Bracey for computer assistance, and The Kitchenware Company, Richmond, Surrey.

Photography
All photographs by Clive Streeter. Additional photography by: Karl Adamson; Martin Brigdale; Philip Dowell; Amanda Heywood; Dave King; David Murray; Stephen Oliver; Susannah Price; Tim Ridley; Jules Selmes; Jerry Young.